Trapped In the Arms Of Death

Overcoming the Grip of Suicide

Dr. Jacquelyn Hadnot

Trapped in the Arms of Death: Overcoming the Grip of Suicide

Unless otherwise indicated, all Scripture quotations are taken from King James Version of the Bible. Copyright © 2000 by AMG Publishers.

Scripture quotations marked AMP are taken from The Amplified Bible AMP. The Amplified Bible, Old Testament copyright © 1965, 1987 by the Zondervan Corporation. The Amplified New Testament, copyright © 1954, 1958, 1987 by the Lockman Foundation. Used by permission.

Please note that Igniting the Fire's publishing style capitalizes certain pronouns in Scripture that refer to the Father, Son, and Holy Spirit, and may differ from some Bible publishers' styles.

Published by Igniting the Fire, Inc.
1314 North 38th Street, Suite 102
Kansas City, KS 66102

Dedication

I dedicate this book to the millions of individuals who live in the shadows of suicide and depression, but who are called to live in the marvelous light. To everyone who has walked in the wilderness of suicide, far too long, and never tasted the Promised Land of abundant life.

To everyone who has gone through the battle with suicide and depression without weapons. To everyone who has been ostracized for having gone through *the valley of the shadow of suicide.* To everyone who has felt the pain or shame of a suicide attempt and was afraid to speak out - you are not alone you are an over comer.

Trapped in the Arms of Death

The Lord God Almighty has heard your cries and seen your tears and He knows that you are holding this book for *"such a time as this."*

I pray that this book will reposition you into your place of divine purpose and destiny and put an end to the cycle of suicidal feelings.

I believe that as you read this book you will come to the revelation that God has not given you the spirit of fear, suicide, or depression - but of power, love and a sound mind.

I pray that you start living a life of passion and purpose for the Lord. A life of passion that is ignited by your deep love for Him. Remember, you are an over comer...

Contents

Trapped in the Arms of Death

INTRODUCTION

What you are about to read is a true story. I did not change the names because it is my story. This is my journey of being a young woman haunted by the spirit of suicide and depression. A story that takes you on my journey of becoming a woman of purpose and destiny.

The Lord is purposely keeping this book short so that you will read it in its entirety. He knows that it is time that you walk in victory.

This is my journey of being trapped in the arms of death and how the Lord broke the grip of suicide over my life.

Trapped in the Arms of Death

CHAPTER 1
TODAY I AM GOING TO DIE...

I sit alone in a cold dark room. On the table before me, a tall glass of water and a bag of pills. No need to leave a note because who would care? Who would understand? As I sit in the cold dark room waiting for the moment to come when I surrender to the spirit that stalks me. I stare at the pills through the tears of hopelessness until the pain of my loneliness and emptiness fills the room.

Trapped in the Arms of Death

I fight back a river of tears while sitting in the cold dark room waiting for the spirit that stalks me to overtake me. I reach for the pills and the tall glass of water that will end the pain and emptiness in my heart. It is at this moment that I know that TODAY I AM GOING TO DIE...

Unless you have experienced the loss of a loved one, the pain of grief will mean nothing to you. For the better part of my life, death was very prevalent. At age five, my paternal grandmother died; age six my maternal grandmother died; age eleven my father was murdered and I watched him being carried way; age fifteen my mother died of a heart attack; age nineteen my best friend was gunned down; age twenty-one a man I loved dearly died. I could go on but I believe this is more than enough to show the path I walked.

Trapped in the Arms of Death

My mother's death caused the worst trauma of all. At 6:30 a.m. I went to my mother's bedroom to awake her for work. I shook the foot of her bed, but she did not respond. I moved to the head of the bed and shook her, but she still did not respond. As I touched her lifeless body, I noticed that she was cold. I continued to shake her, but still no response. I began to cry and reaching for the telephone, called her friend next door. She in turn called an ambulance. When the paramedics arrived they tried to revive her, but my mother was gone. She died during the night from a heart attack at the age of thirty-three.

The pain and anguish you experience when finding a loved one dead is beyond description. The image stays with you for the rest of your life. It reaches a depth of pain inside of you that will last a lifetime. This is where my nightmare begins.

I entered a time warp that would last several years. I did not grieve for my mother because her death was not real to me. I would relive her death repeatedly in my mind.

It was at this point that anguish turned to anger and anger began to fester inside of me because we were uprooted from our lives, our home and everything we knew. Along with my two brothers, Kevin and Greg, we went to live with my maternal grandfather. My brothers also entered a time warp that led them down a road to drugs, prison and eventually death.

We moved to Hayti, Missouri to lived with my

grandfather, a loving and patient man with a heart of gold. Unfortunately, that did not matter to me because anger was soon replaced by rebellion and resentment. As hard as my grandfather tried, he could not reach me. My heart was shattered, bruised, closed and cold, like my cold dark room.

I became extremely rebellious and hard to handle so I went to live with an uncle and his wife. Things did not get any better because it was during this time that the spirit of heaviness (suicide) began to pursue me. I was angry, rebellious and broken and there was no one in my life that could reach me. I was in a very dark place.

To make matters worse I did not feel wanted in my uncle's home. I was in a city with people I did not know. I felt like a stranger in my own skin. I went through the motions of attending school and put on a face of normality, but in reality, I was far from normal. I was on a collision course with destruction and death.

I don't understand why no one sought counseling for us and due to the degree of trauma we experienced we really needed help. It is possible that in those days, it was not commonplace to seek counseling for children - you just moved on with life. I say this because I saw it happen several times in the lives of other children I knew who lost their parents and often the results were the same, dysfunctional kids becoming dysfunctional adults.

I didn't move on and my mother's death was the

tool Satan would use to try to destroy my life - physically and spiritually. To be honest, destroy seems mild in comparison to the things I experienced. [Please note that the enemy is very subtle. He will not pounce on you like a ravenous wolf - he is very methodical in his manipulation and he is patient]. He waits patiently while you fall into his traps and snares. Watch the way he set his trap for a fifteen-year-old child…

Trapped in the Arms of Death

CHAPTER 2
THE TRAP IS SET

I came home from school one afternoon and my uncle's wife was there. I stood outside the door of the apartment and listened to her speak of me over the telephone. Bear in mind, I am a fifteen-year-old child who recently lost her mother. She is telling the listener things I would never say about a child, especially a child in the middle of the pain of grief. It was at that moment that the enemy whispered, "Now is the time."

I knew what he meant. **Now** is the time to prepare to leave this world. "We" had been planning this moment for months. Satan is the master of methodology and manipulation. He knows how to pick the lowest point in your life to invade and deceive you on to a path of self-destruction.

I say [we] began planning because every home I visited meant a visit to their medicine cabinet. I collected pills as if I was on a shopping spree. I never took too many - one or two pills at best. I never took enough to draw attention to my mission. I collected so many pills that I had accumulated enough to fill two bottles. I kept them hidden in my room and collected them without hesitation or reservation. I was on a mission and every medicine cabinet was a step in the direction of my destructive goal - death.

Trapped in the Arms of Death

Satan was about to pull the last straw…

Trapped in the Arms of Death

CHAPTER 3
THE LAST STRAW

The last straw occurred while standing outside the door listening to my aunt tearing me down. I felt so broken by her words and this gave the enemy an open door for me to hear his voice clearly. His words made sense considering no one else would talk to me about my pain. The enemy was there to talk me into a grave of depression and hopelessness. The enemy would say things like:

- ➢ You will not be happy until you are with your mother.
- ➢ These people don't want you here, so you might as well die and by happy again.
- ➢ Do you want to continue to live this way?

The enemy had a long list of lies that made sense to a child in pain and struggling with grief.

For parents reading this book, please know, if you do not talk to your children about the problems they face each day, someone else will and it could mean their destruction - spiritually, physically or emotionally. Sadness, isolation and depression have a way of spiraling out of control.

The enemy had a trap set for me and he was using my family to push the buttons that would drive me to the edge of darkness, heaviness, depression and ultimately suicide. Satan's mission to destroy my destiny was on…

Trapped in the Arms of Death

CHAPTER 4
THE MISSION IS ON

After standing at the door for what seemed like hours, I shook my keys and fumbled with the door in order to give her ample time to change her conversation. As I entered the apartment, she was laughing and talking as if she had no thought of me on her mind or on her lips. I spoke to her, talked for a moment and went upstairs to put away my schoolbooks and begin my journey.

Trapped in the Arms of Death

When you have a mind that is set on suicide, I believe that you may not tell anyone, but the signs are there if someone is paying attention. It is very important to pay attention to a loved one that begins acting in ways that are out of character. Especially children since they can become private and withdrawn. An individual whose heart has given up on living can easily commit the act of suicide if the wrong buttons are pushed. They believe that there is no way out, this can give way to hopelessness, and hopelessness gives way to despair and finally despair gives way to the destructive journey known as suicide.

When a person is gripped by the "spirit of heaviness", every event is magnified one hundred fold. When excessive grief sets in it can lead to depression and ultimately suicidal thoughts. Although some individuals will cry out for help, there will be others that never speak about their pain. So begins my journey into the arms of death...

Trapped in the Arms of Death

CHAPTER 5
MY JOURNEY INTO THE ARMS OF DEATH

When Satan whispered, "It's time" I went to the kitchen and searched for the tallest glass I could find, filled it with water and went back to my room.

My bedroom door had a lock on it - so I locked it because when you are on a secret mission you do not want to be exposed.

I crawled under the bed to retrieve my stash of pills. As I sat on the bed, I thought of writing a note, but **who would care**? **Who would undertand**? Leaving a note seemed like a waste of time, just do it.

I began taking the pills by the hand full. I would consume enough pills to get them down without choking. I swallowed pills until the water ran out. In fact, I still had pills left and no water. I remember thinking if I knew I had collected so many pills, I would have gotten a second glass of water.

When I finished the pills, I got on my knees and ask God to allow me be with my mother. I got into bed and pulled the covers over my head. As I lay in bed in the cold dark room, I began drifting - simply drifting. The tears were trickling down my face as I drifted off to sleep. It was at that moment I thought; today I am going to die.

Trapped in the Arms of Death

CHAPTER 6
IT'S NOT YOUR TIME

The next thing I remember, my aunt was shaking me and screaming, "What have you done?" I was conscious for a moment and replied, "I just want to die."

When I regained consciousness again, I was in an ambulance with paramedics, wires and sirens everywhere. I passed out again.

Trapped in the Arms of Death

The next time I regained consciousness I was in the hospital strapped down to a hospital bed. I laid there thinking, "I am still here." At that moment, I began to cry uncontrollably, but only because I felt I had failed to achieve my mission.

I don't remember how long they kept me because some areas are a little hazy. Finally, a nurse came into the room along with my aunt and uncle to take me to a counselor.

Very subtly, the voice of the enemy said, "They are going to take you to another place, when you get there tell them this was an accident and you will never do it again." The voice then said, "Don't worry, next time we will get it right."

It was at this moment that constant thoughts of

suicide began to control my life through the strongman call "spirit of heaviness." So begins the real journey.

Trapped in the Arms of Death

CHAPTER 7
DEFEATING THE ENEMY OF SUICIDE

It would take several years to defeat the suicidal thoughts that raged through my life. Suicide feeds on depression and depression feeds on suicide. Who can really say which comes first, but I know they go hand in hand.

Once a spirit as strong as suicide has attached

itself to you, it will take the power of God to defeat it. You are not wrestling with flesh and blood; you are wrestling with a spirit. His only mission is to destroy your life.

The only way to defeat the spirit of depression or suicide is through the Spirit of Life - Jesus Christ Jesus said, *"The thief cometh not, but for to steal, and to kill, and to destroy: I am come that they might have life, and that they might have it more abundantly* (John 10:10).

I would attempt to take my life three additional times. The thoughts of suicide raged every time a major or traumatic event happened in my life.

It was not until I surrendered my life to Christ - that the spirit of suicide was defeated. I had to renounce the spirit of suicide in order to be free. I invited destruction into my life the moment I accepted the lies of the enemy and fell victim to his manipulative plan. Suicide is a strong spirit that gains access during times of pain, trauma, sickness, marital problems, death and even drugs.

(I failed to mention that after my mother's death, I began smoking marijuana, drinking, popping pills and anything else I could find to ease the pain and emptiness).

When I gave my life to Christ, the suicidal spirit had no hold over me because Christ now had a hold on me. On the day I DIED to Jacquie and began to LIVE for Christ my life was forever changed. As I began to LIVE FOR CHRIST, He began living in me. No demon on earth can stand in the presence of the Almighty One - El Shaddai.

Suicidal thoughts became a distant memory because Christ Jesus became a reality. When you are engulfed in pain life may seem hopeless, but God is there to see you through!

Jeremiah 29:11 tells us, *"For I know the thoughts that I think toward you, saith the LORD, thoughts of peace, and not of evil, to give you an expected end."* God knows our destiny; we need to get the revelation that we have a destiny in order to defeat the lies of the enemy.

This book was written for everyone, so whether you are a believer or not, the enemy is out to destroy you. Satan is no respecter of persons and he has an open door to your life when you are without a covering. Please get the revelation that without the Lord in your life you are an open target for Satan's destructive arsenal.

Trapped in the Arms of Death

CHAPTER 8
THE REVELATION

In 1999, the Spirit of the Lord instructed me to, *"Get a pen and paper because there is something I want you to know."*

There has always been a question mark in my mind regarding how I got out of the locked room and down a flight of stairs. If you recall, I never mentioned the events that resulted in my aunt finding me. Watch the Lord move!

I was in a locked room, unconscious and dying. The Lord spoke these words in the summer of 1999. He said, *"You tried to take your life, but I carried you to safety because I have work for you to do."* As He spoke, I saw myself being carried down a flight of stairs and being placed on the kitchen floor where my aunt would find me and call for help.

After hearing the Lord's Words and knowing how much He loves me, I burst into tears. The thought that God loves me so much that He sent His angels to carry me to a safe place is beyond description. How amazing is the love of God. I went from being a child trapped in a cyle of helplessness, hopelessness and despair to becoming a woman of purpose and destiny.

It took the Lord twenty-five years to reveal the events of that life-changing day, but it was worth the wait. I now had the answer I so desperately needed to move forward in life. The enemy could not use this piece of my past as an obstacle against me; I was set-free and delivered. No more chains holding me and no more lies from the enemy to trick me into taking my life.

The Lord waited until I was ready to receive the revelation of His love and the length, depth and height of His love towards me. Imagine what He will do for those who are His and called according to His purpose. This kind of love is best described in John 3:16 and Ephesians 3:17-19: *"For God so loved the world, that He gave*

Trapped in the Arms of Death

His only begotten Son, that whoever believes in Him shall not perish, but have eternal life (John 3:16). So that Christ may dwell in your hearts through faith; and that you, being rooted and grounded in love, may be able to comprehend with all the saints what is the breadth and length and height and depth, and to know the love of Christ which surpasses knowledge, that you may be filled up to all the fullness of God" (Ephesians 3:17-19). In order to come to know the fullness of God's love, you must be willing to die...

CHAPTER 9
ANOTHER DEATH...

In 1999 as I lay at the foot of my bed and at the foot of the cross, I knew it was time for another death. This time it was death to the flesh. Jacquie had to die. Die to Jacquie's will and live for Christ and His will. I tried it my way for years and failed. Now it was time to surrender to the One who rescued me from the arms of death.

I attended church regularly, tithed faithfully and

supported every church function, but I had not completely surrendered to Him. I had not given Him what He wanted most - ME. Often, the thing we hold on to can be the thing He wants you to surrender in order to receive His fullness.

Galatians 2:20 says, *"I have been crucified with Christ; and it is no longer I who live, but Christ lives in me; and the life which I now live in the flesh I live by faith in the Son of God, who loved me and gave Himself up for me."*

The day He carried me down the stairs:
❖ I was crucified with Christ.

The day He revealed Himself to me:
❖ It was no longer I who live, but Christ began living in me.

When I surrendered all to Christ:

❖ The life which I now live in the flesh I live by faith in the Son of God who loved me and delivered me from the hand of suicide and delivered Himself up for me.

Therefore, I must die daily to the things that would keep me from receiving the fullness of God. Daily to my own selfish desires. Daily to the human motives that profit nothing. Daily to my self-life issues.

When you walk through the valley of suicide, and walk out victorious you will know that your old self was crucified with Him, that your body of sin might be done away with, that we should no longer be slaves to sin, suicide, depression, drugs, murder, etc. because he who has died is freed from sin.

I am dead to the spirit of suicide; therefore, I am freed from the sin of it. Do not let the sin of … control you - so you would obey its deceptive, enticing lusts. It might sound crazy, but suicide can be enticing because it gives the false impression that you will be free from the pains, trials and tribulations of this world. The devil is a liar! Suicide does not free you - it opens the door for your eternal damnation.

All sin results in death, *"For the wages of sin is death, but the gift of God is eternal life in Christ Jesus our Lord"* (Romans 6:23). When you surrender to the entrapments of sin, *"Do you not know that when you present yourselves to someone as slaves for obedience, you are slaves of the one whom you obey, either of sin resulting in death, or of obedience resulting in righteousness"* (Romans 6:16)?

When I attempted suicide, my flesh was weak and my heart broken by the pain of my mother's death. Grief is a God-given emotion that enables us to cope with feelings that cannot be kept inside, but when we don't let go of the hurt it can become excessive grief and lead to destructive behavior. I became a slave to suicide and it ruled me like a slave master - relentless in his pursuit of my destruction; but where sin increased grace abounded even more in my life. The result, I gave my life to Christ.

Trapped in the Arms of Death

CHAPTER 10
GIVING YOURSELF TO CHRIST

When you surrender ALL to Christ, it will require that you set your heart towards Him. Each day you move forward - you must do so by the Spirit of the Living God. If you do, you will not carry out the desires of the flesh - whatever the desire might be. Any time the thought of suicide tries to raise its ugly head - you will not give place to it because it has been crucified along with its passions and desires that are out to destroy you.

Surrendering to Christ meant that suicide could not trouble me because I bear on my body the brand-mark that reminds me of a cold dark time in my life. A time when the enemy set an obstacle course of suicidal traps before me to keep me from becoming a woman of purpose and destiny. Thanks to God who has given us the victory over the enemy. *"I have been crucified with Christ; and it is no longer I who live, but Christ lives in me; and the life which I now live in the flesh I live by faith in the Son of God, who loved me and gave Himself up for me"* (Galatians 2:20 NASB).

I now live a victorious life through Christ Jesus. Same view different room...

CHAPTER 11
A ROOM WITH A VIEW

I now sit in a light filled room. Placed before me on the table, a tall endless glass of living water (Jesus Christ) and a plate of bread (the Word of God). In them, I find life, peace, joy, contentment and love. Jesus said of the living water, *"If anyone is thirsty, let him come to Me and drink. "He who believes in Me, as the Scripture said, 'From his innermost being will flow rivers of living water.'"* (John 7:37-38). Jesus also said to them, *"I am the bread of life; he who comes to Me will not hunger, and he who believes in Me will never thirst"* (John 6:35).

Who Cares? I wrote this book because I care and Jesus cares. He desires that not another soul fall prey to the bait of Satan and the temptation of suicide. **Who will understand?** Anyone who has ever contemplated or attempted suicide. Because I contemplated and attempted suicide, I understand. Jesus said, *"I am come that they might have life, and that they might have it more abundantly"* (John 10:10).

Choose life. I did and I am forever grateful that Jesus gave his angels charge over me to keep me from dashing my foot on the stone of suicide.

Trapped in the Arms of Death

Again, choose life because a life in Christ is a life filled with beauty and splendor regardless of the trials and tribulations we face. When Jesus is on your side you are more than a conqueror and you are an over comer by the blood of the Lamb and by the word of your testimony.

My testimony is written within the pages of this book and I am an over comer - I overcame the bondage of suicide and depression to become a woman of purpose and destiny and I owe it all to Jesus Christ who loved me enough to save me from a cold dark room. I owe Him everything and I plan to spend every day of my life showing Him how much I appreciate the gift of life He gave me. Opening up and being transparent about a painful time in my life is a small price to pay for the great price He paid for me.

Live in His light, love in His light. Someone needs to know that you are an over comer, so they too can overcome. We are more than conquerors through Christ Jesus. Let's die to self and live for Christ so that we can be seated with Him.

CHAPTER 12
SEATED WITH CHRIST

"I am crucified with Christ: nevertheless I live; yet not I, but Christ liveth in me: and the life which I now live in the flesh I live by the faith of the Son of God, who loved me, and gave himself for me" (Galatians 2:20 KJV).

"I have been crucified with Christ [in Him I have shared His crucifixion]; it is no longer I who live, but Christ (the Messiah) lives in me; and the

life I now live in the body I live by faith in (by adherence to and reliance on and complete trust in) the Son of God, Who loved me and gave Himself up for me" (Galatians 2:20 AMP).

Let's look at Galatians 2:20, the Apostle Paul states that he has died to the law so that he might live for God. This is true because he has been united to the Lord Jesus Christ. Jesus died; so did Paul. Jesus rose again; so did Paul. Jesus Christ died; so did I.

Having died and come to life in Christ, we actually take part in Christ's death and resurrection, conceived because of the spiritual unification with the Lord.

Trapped in the Arms of Death

What does it mean to be "in Christ"? It means being joined to Christ and the experiences of Christ become our experiences. Therefore, his death for sin was our death; his resurrection was our resurrection; his ascension was our ascension, so that we are seated with Christ "in the heavenly realms." When we died with Christ, our "old self" died with Christ.

Paul adds that the life he lives now is lived "by faith." It is a different life from the life in which he was striving to be justified by the law. In another sense, it is not Paul who is living, but rather Christ who lives in him. It is not us living, but Christ living in us.

Live in His light, love in His light because Jesus is the light of the world. Then Jesus again spoke to them, saying, *"I am the Light of the world; he who follows Me will not walk in the darkness, but will have the Light of life"* (John 8:12).

CHAPTER 13
RECOGNIZING THE ENEMY

It is vital to recognize the enemy that seeks to destroy your life. Whoever the enemy is, he has a name. Identify him so that he can be destroyed. The enemy trying to destroy me was called, the spirit of heaviness. Isaiah 61:3 tells us, *"To appoint unto them that mourn in Zion, to give unto them beauty for ashes, the oil of joy for mourning, the garment of praise for the* **spirit of** *heaviness; that they might be called trees of righteousness, the planting of the LORD, that he might be glorified"* (KJV).

In order to defeat your enemy you must recognize him and his symptoms. Symptoms of this destructive enemy include depression, severe mourning, anguish, misery, hopelessness, grief, sorrow, loneliness, fear, torment, restlessness, self-pity, discontent, and sleeplessness. Because of the emptiness inside, I also became a regular gambler because I needed to fill the empty places in my life. For whatever strange reason, sitting at a slot machine was mind numbing and gave way to hours of mindless escape. Who knew it was another trap of the enemy? Satan will use whatever tool is available to entrap you.

Trapped in the Arms of Death

Drs. Jerry and Carol Robeson tell us in Strongman's His Name…What's His Game tells us, *"The spirit of heaviness tries to take our joy of living by loading us down with heaviness. He attempts to move in when we are mourning and keep us in an abnormal state of perpetual grief."*[1]

We must bind the enemy and begin walking out the healing process. Isaiah tells us that Jesus bore our grief in Isaiah 53:4, but He cannot bear or carry it when we will not let go. Just as extreme mourning led to many destructive years in my life, the same will happen if you continue to carry the pains of grief on your heart. I didn't know that Jesus was waiting to carry my grief and as a result, I suffered many agonizing years needlessly.

Trapped in the Arms of Death

Grief is an emotion that allows us to empty out our feelings of hurt and pain and it must be allowed to run it's course if we are going to lead a healthy and productive life.

I caused myself great harm when I denied the grieving process and only delayed the inevitable - mourning the loss of my mother. The emotional trauma you experience because of denial is just as devastating as the loss itself. It can cause severe neurosis and ultimately a disconnection with reality.

We must learn to address the problems that open the door to depression, heaviness, sadness, and ultimately suicide.

Depression is at an all time high due to failed

marriages, finances and a failing economy, peer pressures, death, drugs, unemployment and much more. The National Institute of Mental Health says one in every five Americans, 40 million people, have significant symptoms of depression at any one time. About 2.4 million of them suffer severe clinical depression.[2]

We must recognize the spirits of heaviness, depression and suicide for what they are, enemies that are out to destroy life. Jesus said in John 10:10, *"The thief cometh not, but for to steal, to kill, and to destroy: I am come that they might have life, and that they might have it more abundantly."*

Therefore based on Isaiah 61:3 Jesus came to:
➢ grant consolation and joy to those who mourn.

➢ give them an ornament of beauty instead of ashes.

➢ give the oil of joy instead of mourning.

➢ give the garment of praise instead of a heavy, burdened, and failing spirit.

He did it so that we may be called oaks of righteousness [lofty, strong, and magnificent, distinguished for uprightness, justice, and right standing with God], the planting of the Lord, that He may be glorified (AMP).

Praise or the garment of praise is very effective in defeating the spirit of heaviness. When we praise God, the focus shifts off us and onto God. Praise says, "I have my heart and mind focused on Jesus because the joy of the Lord is my strength." He is our strength, a present help in times of trouble. As we focus on our Lord Jesus, He will show us the way to defeat the enemy of depression and heaviness.

Even if you don't feel like praising God, I encourage you to press in and praise Him in spite of everything around you. When you press in to God, He will meet you in the midst of your praise. Psalm 22:3 tells us that He inhabits the praises of His people. As He inhabits your praise, He will cover you with his feathers, and under his wings, you will find refuge.

Depression and heaviness are strong enemies (notice I did not say powerful enemies), I believe that is why they are considered strongmen, but they are not stronger than our Lord and Savior

Jesus Christ who defeated death on the cross. *"O DEATH, WHERE IS YOUR VICTORY? O DEATH, WHERE IS YOUR STING?" The sting of death is sin, and the power of sin is the law; but thanks be to God, who gives us the victory through our Lord Jesus Christ"* (1Corinthians 15:55-57).

We have the victory through Christ Jesus. Just as He carried me down the stairs to safety, He wants to carry you. In the safety of His arms, you will find rest and answers to the problems that have weighed you down and brought you to the point of helplessness and hopelessness. He is waiting - JUST FOR YOU.

"Nay, in all these things we are more than conquerors through him that loved us. For I am

persuaded, that neither death, nor life, nor angels, nor principalities, nor powers, nor things present, nor things to come, Nor height, nor depth, nor any other creature, shall be able to separate us from the love of God, which is in Christ Jesus our Lord."

Romans 8:37-39

You are more than a conqueror through Christ Jesus. Walk in victory because you are an over comer by the precious Blood of the Lamb and you will defeat the spirit of suicide, fear, depression, heaviness, and every demonic force that tries to come against you. WALK IN VICTORY.

Trapped in the Arms of Death

CHAPTER 14
DISCOVERING THE
BUTTERFLY IN YOU

I like to think of myself as a butterfly because of the life changing metamorphosis of a butterfly. A butterfly starts out as a caterpillar, which is a young insect or worm with a long soft body, many short legs, and often brightly colored or spiny skin. It crawls along making his way through life. The caterpillar's due season arrives and it is time to begin the journey of becoming the beautiful new creature God created him to be. The caterpillar begins spinning a cocoon (*the silky covering with which a caterpillar or other insect larva encloses itself during its transition to an adult state*) in which to enclose himself or to hide himself from the world. As the caterpillar is suspended within the cocoon, changes are occurring that will birth out a new creature very unrecognizable to the world. Chemical adjustments are made to his DNA, bodily functions change, even the thought process begins to change. I believe that the mind of the caterpillar must be renewed if he is going to function to the fullest of his potential. Otherwise, the new butterfly would be crawling around on the ground trying to find his destiny.

Once the caterpillar has been hidden in the

cocoon for the designated period of time, his due season arrives and he begins the ardent task of being birthed out of the cocoon. Slowly the cocoon releases the new creation to the world. A new creature emerges from the cocoon ready to greet the world and begin his new life.

Although his process is not complete, he knows that a change has occurred. Because of the new mindset, the caterpillar instinctively knows that there is still work to be done in and through him if he is going to receive all that God has for him.

He then finds a place in which to allow the sun to dry his wings and strengthen his heart for his new journey. He sits perched as the sun prepares him for his new season in life. Once his wings are dry and blood has filled them properly, the butterfly is now ready to fly.

The new creation emerges with beauty and splendor. With strong wings, the butterfly can soar to the highest heights. The destiny before him is great because he can fly to places caterpillars only see in their dreams. The butterfly is the ultimate idea of man's transformation in the spirit.

Imagine you are a caterpillar, crawling your way out of suicidal thoughts, drugs, alcohol, sexual promiscuity, sexual abuse, spousal abuse, depression, un-forgiveness, fear, doubt, unbelief or another of Satan's evil fruit. Before we surrendered our lives to Christ, we were like the caterpillar, crawling around trying to find our way. After we surrendered to the Lord, He began to spin a spiritual cocoon in which to hide us from the hand of the enemy so He could do a work in us. He began to change our spiritual DNA to reflect His DNA in mind, heart and spirit. He filled us with His Word as He showed us His great love and tender care. He protected us from the hand of the enemy as he began to mold us into the beautiful image He pre-destined for us. While we are in the cocoon, he changes our mindset so that we can begin to walk in the fullness of life. He changes our heart so that it is strong and sure. He places within us a desire to soar for the Kingdom of God. He purges out old habits and desires that caused us to crawl through life settling for less than His best.

Once the process is complete, we emerge from our spiritual cocoon a new creature in Christ

Jesus. However, He is not finished with us. He then places us on a windowsill in order to allow the "SON" to dry our spiritual wings and strengthen our hearts to go the distance in life. He does not want us to come off the sill too soon because wet wings could mean disaster. A weak heart could mean we fall prey to the devices of the enemy. In other words, if we come off the windowsill too soon we could do more harm to ourselves and fail to reach our full potential. Too many believers get in a hurry, leave the sill or shelf before they are ready, and miss being "dried" or "tried" by the Lord.

The Lord once told me, *"I am taking my time with you so that you do not fall prey to pride and greed and fail."* After seeing so many powerful men and women of God fall prey to the bait of

Trapped in the Arms of Death

Satan through sexual immorality, greed, perversions, drugs and the like - I understand completely and I am grateful that the Lord loves me so much that He did now allow me to move off the shelf too soon. He kept me hidden until the time came when He knew that my wings were strong and my heart was sure in Him. The Lord needs strong men and women who will stand in the midst of the battle and not fall prey to the snares of the enemy. Money won't be a trap to shut down the uncompromising message of Jesus Christ. We won't form one hundred dollar lines that cause people to feel inadequate because they can't afford to give. We won't have moneymaking schemes and moneychangers in the house of God.

The Lord needs men and women who will trust

God for the provision of the ministry and allow Him to lead and guide them into all truths.

We won't build bigger buildings; instead, we will build up people to walk in the fullness of Christ. We won't just preach prosperity; we will show God's people how to walk in prosperity through the renewing of their minds. We will hunger and thirst for the things that give Him glory. We will hunger for more of Him. When God is in your future - all limits are off.

Finally, when God **is** your future, your desire for Him will far out weigh your desire for notoriety, ministry, power or position. He will be your ultimate passion. You might ask what this has to do with overcoming depression or suicidal thoughts. The answer, I believe, is often when we fail to meet our self made plans and goals, we unknowingly open a door for the enemies traps and snares. When you allow the Lord to birth you out of your cocoon and into the fullness of His plans for you, there is no place for the devil. Again, when God is your future - you have no limits.

Trapped in the Arms of Death

Chapter 15
Conclusion

We have come to the end of our journey. I pray that you have been encouraged, inspired and motivated through my testimony. You are an over comer and according to the power of God that works in and through you - you can over come the traps of the enemy to walk in the fullness of life.

The Apostle Paul said in Ephesians 3:20: "*Now*

unto him that is able to do exceeding abundantly above all that we ask or think, according to the power that worketh in us." Through Christ Jesus, we have the power to walk in exceeding abundantly and above all that we ask or think. What power is working in you?

Is it the power to over come the spirit of depression and suicide? Is it the power to over come the lies, snares and deception of the enemy? Is it the power to say I am an over comer by the blood of the Lamb and by the word of my testimony? Is it the power to come out of your cocoon and begin to fly like the beautiful butterfly God created you to be?

My friend, it is possible to walk in the fullness of God's love, purpose and destiny. Even though the enemy tries to tell you the opposite, please know that with God all things are possible.

Overcoming the pains of your past is a journey that you will travel in your lifetime, but it is possible as long as you are sheltered in the arms of Christ Jesus. Allow Him to be your shield and shelter - your strong tower against your enemies.

For thou hast been a shelter for me, and a strong tower from the enemy. Psalm 61:3

The name of the LORD is a strong tower: the righteous runneth into it, and is safe.
Proverbs 18:10

We should have a heart like that of King David when he was overwhelmed and faint, he cried out to the Lord. When your heart is overwhelmed with the cares of this world, your prayer should be - lead me to the rock that is higher than I. *"HEAR MY cry, O God; listen to my prayer. From the end of the earth will I cry to You, when my heart is overwhelmed and fainting; lead me to the rock that is higher than I [yes, a rock that is too high for me]. For You have been a shelter and a refuge for me, a strong tower against the adversary. I will dwell in our tabernacle forever; let me find refuge and trust in the shelter of Your wings."* (Psalm 61:1-4).

Beloved, allow the Lord to show you the fullness of His love as you grow in Him. Beautiful butterfly of the Lord live in the "Son" Light and be blessed.

BINDING THE SPIRIT OF SUICIDE AND HEAVINESS

Heavenly Father, I come to You in the Name of my Lord and Savior Christ Jesus. Holy Spirit I pray that You will quicken me to hear my Heavenly Father's Voice and to lead me in prayer. Heavenly Father, I bow down and worship before You. I come to You with praise and with thanksgiving. I come to you in humility, in fear, in trembling and seeking truth. I come to You in gratitude, in love, and through the precious Blood of Your Son Jesus Christ.

Trapped in the Arms of Death

Satan, in the Name of Jesus I bind your Strongman called spirit of heaviness and suicide. I bind your spirit in the Name of Jesus Christ according to Matthew 18:18 that promises, *'...whatever ye shall bind on earth shall be bound in heaven:'* along with all your works, roots, fruits, links and spirits that are in my life and send them back to hell. In the Name of Jesus.

Lord Jesus, I ask You to destroy any familiar spirit that has allowed any of these demonic strongmen into my presence. In the Name of Jesus Christ according to John 14:14.

Heavenly Father, I ask You to loose into me: the Spirit of Adoption (Romans 8:15), the Spirit of Truth (1 John 4:6, Psalm 51:10), the Holy Spirit of Truth (John 16:13), the Spirit of Resurrection

Life and life more Abundantly (John 11:25), (John 10:10b), the Holy Spirit and His Gifts (1 Cor. 12:9-12). In the Name of Jesus. Amen.

Trapped in the Arms of Death

PRAYER OF SALVATION

No matter what you do in life, nothing else will matter except your relationship with Jesus Christ. A committed relationship with Jesus is the key to a victorious life. Our Lord and Savior laid down His life for us. He rose again for us so that we could spend eternity with Him. Jesus said, *"I am come that they might have life, and that they might have it more abundantly."*

It is God's will that everyone receive eternal salvation. The only way to receive salvation is to call upon the name of Jesus and confess Him as Lord of your life. The Bible says in Romans 10: 9-13, that if thou shalt confess with thy mouth the Lord Jesus, and shalt believe in thine heart that God hath raised him from the dead, thou shalt be saved. *For with the heart man believeth unto righteousness; and with the mouth, confession is made unto salvation. For the scripture saith, whosoever believeth on him shall not be ashamed. For there is no difference between the Jew and the Greek: for the same*

Trapped in the Arms of Death

Lord over all is rich unto all that call upon him. For whosoever shall call upon the name of the Lord shall be saved.

God loves you, no matter who you are, no matter what your past. God loves you so much that He gave His one and only begotten Son for you. The Bible tells us *"...whoever believes in him shall not perish but have eternal life"* (John 3:16 NIV). Jesus laid down His life and rose again so that we could spend eternity with Him in heaven and experience His absolute best on earth. If you would like to receive Jesus into your life, say the following prayer aloud. It is vital that you mean it from your heart.

> *Heavenly Father, I come to You admitting that I am a sinner. Right now, I choose to turn away from sin, and I ask You to cleanse me of all unrighteousness. I believe that Your Son, Jesus, died on the cross to take away my sins. I also believe that He rose again from the dead so that I may be justified and made righteous through faith*

in Him. I call upon the name of Jesus Christ to be the Savior of my life. Jesus, I choose to follow You, and I ask that You fill me with the power of the Holy Spirit. I declare right now that I am a born-again child of God. I am free from sin, and full of the righteousness of God. I am saved in Jesus' name. Amen.

If you prayed this prayer to receive Jesus Christ as your Lord and Savior or if this book has blessed your life, we would like to hear from you. Please write us:

Igniting the Fire Publishing
1314 North 38th Street, Suite 101
Kansas City, KS 66102
Or
It Is Written Ministries
1314 North 38th Street, Suite 102
Kansas City, KS 66102

Trapped in the Arms of Death

Meet Dr. Jacquie

The Author

Dr. Jacquelyn Brown-Hadnot is an author and teacher whose passion is to teach the bible in a way that changes lives. She has written several books such as the award winning *Cry Aloud, Spare Not! A Prophetic Call to the Fast God Has Chosen for You*, which received the 2007 Indie Excellence Finalist Award and USA Book News 2006 Best General Religion Book of the Year; Cry Aloud, Spare Not! The Companion Study Guide; His Mercy Endures Forever: Psalms, Prayers & Meditations for the Heart; To Make War with the Saints: Satan's Kingdom Agenda; A Treasure in the Pleasure of Loving God and other print and audio books.

The Overseer

It is her great love for the Body of Christ that prompted Jacquie to birth It Is Written Ministries, Inc. It Is Written Ministries is a unique non-profit ministry that endeavors to encourage, motivate, and educate individuals to walk in wisdom, character, and holiness. It Is Written feeds the triune man; mind, body and spirit through outreaches such as food and clothing pantries, nursing home outreaches, meals to the homeless and teaching ministries on foundations for victorious Christian living, biblical financial principles, prayer and worship.

She holds a Doctorate in Pastoral Theology, a Masters in Ministry Leadership and Bachelors in Theology.

The Teacher/Speaker

Dr. Jacquie is a frequently requested speaker for churches, women's groups, general audiences, and seminars for independent gospel artists, biblical financial principals, fasting, prayer and worship.

She is the founder of the Agape Learning Center, an outreach of It Is Written Ministries. The learning center was founded to provide a quality education to individuals with a desire to grow in their personal lives, but cannot afford a traditional education.

Jacquie has also made television appearances on such shows as Lift Him up Kansas, TBN Praise The Lord, and Soldiers for Jesus Christ, Joy Night Television and several others. She is also the host of *Light for Your Path* and *The Heart of a Psalmist* radio broadcasts that air nationally and internationally in more than 56 countries, 80+ cities.

The Psalmist

Jacquie flows under a powerful psalmist and prophetic anointing causing her to be an effective vessel for the Kingdom of God. Jacquie is a Spoken Word Psalmist and her CD "His Mercy Endures Forever" has received nationwide airplay, 2006 Newsome Award for Spoken Word of the Year, 2005 Joy Night Music Award for Best Worship Music, 2005 Omer Award for Spoken Word of the Year, 2006 Momentum Award nomination and 2006 Just Plain Folks nomination. She has released two additional worship projects, The Spoken Word of Love and The Extravagant Love of God.

Jacquie frequently ministers music where she speaks. As a psalmist, music is a vital part of worship and Jacquie uses music as a way to connect to the heart of God's people.

The Entrepreneur

Jacquie and her husband Minister Gregory Hadnot launched Igniting the Fire Media Group in 2006 that includes:

- ➤ ITF Publishing
- ➤ ITF Records
- ➤ GLORI Radio
- ➤ ITF Television

Jacquie has been the President and CFO of The Diversified Group, Inc. an accounting and income preparation firm for over twenty-six years.

Jacquie and Minister Gregory have been married for over ten years and together they oversee It Is Written Ministries. They reside in Overland Park, KS. She has one daughter, Jacquanda and a grandson, Tristan.

Trapped in the Arms of Death

Other Books & Materials by Dr. Jacquie

Books in Print
- The Extravagant Love of God: Experiencing the Prophetic Flow
- Cry Aloud, Spare Not! A Prophetic Call to the Fast God Has Chosen
- Cry Aloud, Spare Not! The Companion-Study Guide
- His Mercy Endures Forever: Psalms, Prayers & Meditations
- To Make War with the Saints; Satan's Kingdom Agenda
- A Treasure in the Pleasure of Loving God
- Loving God through His Names: 365 Days of the Year
- Closing the Doors to Satan's Attacks: *Overcoming Fear*
- Where Is Your God? Have We Lost the Referential Fear of the Lord?

Audio Books & Teachings
- More of You… (Volume 1)
- In the Face of Adversity: *Overcoming Life's Storms*
- Be Not Deceived…
- Where Is Your God?
- Recognizing Your Due Season
- Praying the Healing Scriptures
- The Enemy in Me: *Overcoming Self-Life Issues*

Music
- The Extravagant Love of God
- His Mercy Endures Forever: Praying the Psalms
- The Spoken Word of Love

Trapped in the Arms of Death

For More Information:
www.jacquiehadnot.com or www.ignitingthefire.net
Or write us:
jacquie@jacquiehadnot.com

Trapped in the Arms of Death

Trapped in the Arms of Death

[1] Strongman's His Name What's His Game, Drs. Jerry and Carol Robeson, pp 50.

[2] Strongman's His Name What's His Game, Drs. Jerry and Carol Robeson, pp 52.

www.ingramcontent.com/pod-product-compliance
Lightning Source LLC
Chambersburg PA
CBHW070205290526
45789CB00002B/924